NO MORE BREAKUP

EXPOSED: The secret behind a long lasting relationship and marriage.

By Joseph Blunt

Table of contents

Chapter 1

HAVING EFFECTIVE COMMUNICATION

Correspondence is the reason for a solid relationship or marriage. It's the way you and your mate interface, share your considerations and perspectives, and resolve debates. Relationship relational abilities don't come simple for everybody. A few couples should deal with their strategies for quite a long time. However, over the long run, they will actually want to talk straightforwardly and sincerely with each other.

Regardless of how associated you and your life partner are currently, there is consistently space to reinforce and develop your relationship. Here are the significant hints to assist you with building an adoration MORE and battle LESS procedure in your relationship or marriage.

- Being self awareness

Step by step instructions to Improve Your Relationship By Focusing Inward.

A large portion of us have a sensible thought of what mindfulness is - a comprehension and knowledge into our own interior world, and responses. One approach to characterizing mindfulness could really be taking a gander at what it isn't and we can now and then see individuals who are totally careless in regards to what is happening inside. This can appear as though somebody who is receptive, inclined to projection, unreliable, guarded and unfit to get a sense of ownership with their own issues - and who might battle to feel fulfilled and content in their lives by and large. A large portion of us exist on a range of mindfulness, for certain individuals profoundly fixed on their inward universes, and others totally unmindful yet it is a valuable idea to ponder.

One aspect of our lives where mindfulness is practically fundamental is seeing someone - whether this is heartfelt or dispassionate. In the event that we are capable of what's going on for us genuinely and intellectually, it tends to be a lot simpler to recognize issues that have come up. For instance, sensations of outrage at our accomplice for being late home can be better perceived as frailty, and we can de-raise what is happening by advising ourselves that we're probably answering recollections of a past relationship.

Feeling irate at a companion for requesting a great deal within recent memory can be perceived as sensations of culpability and of being conflicted between needing to help the companion, yet additionally requiring that much-treasured alone chance to unwind.

So presently we've laid out that mindfulness is a key relationship device. How might we ensure we have fostered this ability, and that we are utilizing it for our potential benefit? Here are a few valuable tips:

Therapy

For some individuals, the method involved with looking for treatment whether this is relationship treatment or individual is an undeniable mindful dark hole. Regardless of whether you just look for help for uneasiness or stress, a huge piece of the course of treatment includes inspecting our previous encounters and perceiving how they have molded us, and how our contemplations and sentiments cross.

This can be an exceptionally helpful cycle on the off chance that you're needing to see more about your own inspirations and conduct and specialists are prepared to pose the right inquiries and convey those 'epiphanies. For instance, in talking through your past selections of accomplices, you could find a propensity to pick depressed accomplices, or the people who are probably not going to hurt you - prompting another familiarity with your inward inspirations, and the valuable chance to do things any other way sometime later.

Mindful Meditation

You've probably heard every one of the narratives and proposals for care and reflection - and fortunately the vast majority of these are right on target.

Care specifically is perfect for creating mindfulness, since we are offered the chance to tune in with ourselves and switch off from interruptions. Many individuals report enhancements in their connections when they practice care, since they are more mindful of what's going on for them inside, can find opportunity to tune in, and can pick how they respond. For instance, on the off chance that I were busy moving house and something unpleasant or disturbing occurred with a relative, I could see myself beginning to blow up, and settle on the choice to step away quickly.

Since care urges us to see how feelings feel in our bodies, we can be considerably more responsive to the actual experience of feelings - whether this is a snugness in our chests or holding in our stomach flagging nervousness, or a fixing or our jaw or shivering in our grasp flagging pressure or outrage.

Coaching

A less extreme method for creating mindfulness is through training whether this is relationship instructing or person. Very much like specialists, mentors are prepared to pose the 'right' inquiries yet these are many times more based around your qualities and objectives throughout everyday life.

Many individuals who have had instruction will portray themselves as more purposeful and careful than previously, and will feel associated with their inward drive and inspiration; they will have explained their objectives and how these will assist them with accomplishing their desired relationship.

Training frequently assists individuals with associating with their 10,000 foot view, and raises their attention to how their everyday lives add to this.

Journaling

Who knows what goes on inside our heads most of the time? Many people have a long, internal monologue that is sorting through our day to day lives and many of our behaviors and thoughts might be almost automatic and unconscious (especially things like checking our phones or daydreaming about this and that).

Journaling is a free and relaxing way to get some of those thoughts out on paper and reflect on what is happening both inside and outside our heads. Just like therapy raises our self awareness when we are given space to talk things through, journaling provides a similar space and best of all, you can read back over what you've written. Most of us don't take the opportunity to do this in our day to day lives, but if we can develop a habit of daily journaling, it often becomes a valuable resource in alerting us to issues or gaps in our lives.

Did you know?Journaling is a form of self-care. Get relationship self care tips, customized lesson plans, interactive quizzes and more with Relish.

Sharing feelings

This may not really shock or amaze anyone, rather one of the most outstanding ways of turning out to be more mindful is to start imparting things to others whether this is your accomplice or companions. At the point when we discuss what's going on for us, we additionally welcome others to share their encounters and through hearing their accounts, we can likewise think about our own.

Innovation can assist with sharing our contemplations or sentiments about things in the relationship. It is a capability which urges individuals to impart their considerations and recollections to their accomplice to fabricate trust and association, as well as posing interesting inquiries.

Alternate approaches to incorporating this training into day to day existence: remember a night out where you center for examining the 'enormous' points (like qualities, your future, and closeness), or put away a period before bed to talk as the days progressed and share your difficulties and wins. Analysts have found that taking stock of what went well every day, and why, assists with mind-set and prosperity and it is additionally liable to assist with self-and-accomplice mindfulness, since you'll be imparting this to one another.

- Listening to your partner

These issues can seem like a little or funny thing, yet they're entirely key side effects that could bring about profound detachment, hatred and floating separated. Profound listening can help. Listening IS troublesome! Be that as it may, don't settle, we can ALL get to the next level.

WHY IS LISTENING SO HARD?

It's not unexpected a consequence of molding, and not genuinely the way in which you need to answer one another (and cause each other to feel)

Here are the significant necessities you want to be aware of and why paying attention to your accomplice is vital and furthermore assists you with building serious areas of strength for an in your relationship.

Listening requires fixation:

Most likely, undivided attention is truly requesting! Our mind is now attempting to process such countless complex pictures, sounds, and data all while working a whole body! It takes a great deal of training and concentration to listen intentionally. Begin by just rewording what's being said and verifying whether you're on target.

Listening requires opposing driving forces:

Rather than "tuning in", it's not unexpected to contemplate our reaction, our conveyance and by and large the way that we will run over to the next person. It's difficult to suspend our "internal" center.

Listening expects that we suspend critical thinking:

We're wired to see issues and to fix or keep away from them. This intends that rather than profoundly paying attention to the next individual, we're quite tackling and breaking down. All things considered, inquire as to whether they're shifting focus over to issue settle or basically to vent or be heard.

Listening requires non-judgment:

Particularly when somebody is grumbling about you, your thoughts, or something you did, you could feel learned to guard yourself or to make your own statement of view... Unfortunately that is not listening by the same token. All things considered, tenderly request that they use "I" proclamations so you can really hear what the issues are as opposed to feeling protective.

Primary concern: time and again we answer and respond excessively fast in circumstances, particularly when our accomplices are simply attempting to be heard and feel seen. They attempt to fix, issue, settle, judge, express guidance and impressions, and take up a position before really sitting with their accomplice's existence and their internal world.

THE RESULT OF POOR LISTENING?

You accidentally invalid each other's sentiments. This is where numerous connections go wrong. But you can definitely relax, we have you covered.

To construct a flourishing relationship, transform each discussion into an act of profound cognizant tuning in. This will work on your feeling of association and capacity to share and approve each other's sentiments.

DON'T KNOW WHERE TO START?

Indeed, on the off chance that you're focused on your relationship, execute these abilities immediately to have that flourishing relationship you merit:

1. Listen to learn, not to answer.

Truly pay attention to what your accomplice is talking about and, surprisingly, more eagerly for what they're feeling. Can't hear it? Ask interest based inquiries like:

"Is there a story behind this for you?"

"Might this connect with a worth of yours?"

"What's generally disturbing to you about this?"

If all else fails, essentially start an inquiry with all things considered "who", "what", "where", "how", "when", "why", or "how".

Also, to recollect, it's OK to be urged to say "I don't have the foggiest idea", or to embrace the quiet. Keep in mind, this isn't an exhibition and you're not being evaluated. This is about human association and we're intricate creatures.

Your most memorable assignment is to become totally clear about their perspective, whether you concur with it.

2. Rehash to recognize, not to really look at a case.

There are two sections to doing this. The superficial part is to in a real sense repeat what you heard them say regarding their experience and feeling:

"I heard you say [...] And that it caused you to feel [...] Is that right?"

This could take different back and forths and that is ordinary. It's anything but a contest to see who can accomplish understanding the quickest. It's likewise not a potential chance to pass judgment on your accomplice in the event that they struggle with grasping you.

Its further part is to really associate with their feeling(s). You'll in a real sense their help when you can associate with what your accomplice is talking about and feeling.

Regardless of whether you concur with what they're saying or can't connect with their experience, the odds are you can recall what is going on in which you felt what they're feeling (for example culpability, misfortune, disappointment). In the event that not, just envision what it might be to want to feel what they're feeling. At the point when you do this, your affirmation will be certified, genuine, and credible.

3, Ask what they need most. When your accomplice says and feels that you truly get it, ask what they could have to move forward:

"What is it that you really want? "Is there anything I can do to help you in this?"

Welcome them to talk and to share. Propose to assist them with investigating/conceptualizing provided that they need your help. In a flourishing relationship, we really want to tune in, learn and forget prior to making the fitting moves TOGETHER. At the point when you do this right, you'll be "holding space" for your accomplice.

WHAT DOES HOLDING SPACE LOOK LIKE?

Holding space means sitting with their reality and making the moment about them, without trying to convince, fix or judge. It sounds like:

"I hear you", because I'm asking clarifying questions about your thoughts and feelings.

It feels like:

"I see you", because I'm validating your lived experience with no intent to fix or judge.

It's actually like:

"I'm with you", because I'm simply choosing to connect with what you're feeling, even if I might disagree or have

- Building trust and emotional intimacy

At the point when we examine closeness in a heartfelt relationshipship, what ordinarily strikes a chord are actual demonstrations, like clasping hands, nestling, kissing and even sex. While actual closeness is basic in any heartfelt organization, one of the essential elements separates it from some other sort of relationship encouraging profound closeness is similarly as, while perhaps not more, significant.

WHAT IS EMOTIONAL INTIMACY AND WHY DOES IT MATTER?

Profound closeness could be characterized as permitting yourself to interface all the more profoundly with your accomplice through activities that express sentiments, weaknesses and trust. Part of a relationship is sharing your mysteries, discussing your relationship, and telling your accomplice significant news. A couple is by and large more joyful when the two players can share and see each other's sentiments.

Eventually, close to home closeness makes a profound conviction that all is good inside your relationship and a capacity to be completely yourself imperfections and everything without feeling as though you risk the actual relationship. Without this closeness, a relationship battles in numerous ways.

For instance, you could feel harsh or angry, experience extreme touchiness, have fears with respect to your accomplice's unwaveringness to you, or experience sensations of detachment or dejection.

On the off chance that close to home closeness is missing, [one or both of you] may feel an absence of wellbeing, love, support, in general association, and it likewise will no doubt influence the actual closeness in a heartfelt connection.

Trust:

What's so difficult to construct, simple to destroy, and significant to any sound close connection? Trust. Your association might begin with a meet-charming and a flash, yet for a relationship to have genuine backbone, you must have the option to utilize the "T" word while portraying how you feel about your accomplice.

On the off chance that you need a sound, blissful, long haul relationship, you'll have to focus on building and keeping up with trust,

Without it, different things like profound closeness and association can't get sorted out.

Like a great deal of significant things throughout everyday life, building trust doesn't simply occur. It takes work that adds up to substantially more than a couple of those falling activities from secondary school. In any case, the outcome is such a ton better. First of all, you'll have a real sense of reassurance in what you have, realize your individual won't plunge when things get messed up, and have a good sense of security, embraced, and genuinely cherished.

The terrible news is that trust is something fragile. Everybody comes into associations with their own past chronicles, including those where trust might have been broken before. Notwithstanding, even with all that could have happened earlier, you ought to realize that it's as yet feasible for you to have, all things considered, trust in your relationship. "I generally believe it's smarter to take the jump and trust someone until they show you they're not dependable.

"Trust" can be deciphered in different ways by various individuals, and it's generally expected to be something that you're not ready to depict until you feel it. You know when you trust your accomplice and you positively know when you don't.

"Trust is the sensation of close to home, physical, and mental security created when an individual is predictable with their way of behaving, Answering the subject of "do you trust your accomplice" comes down to the amount you feel you will be upheld by that individual if/when you really want them.

Beyond feeling like you can believe what they say, you need to have the option to know that assuming you really want something regardless of how enormous or little you can depend on your S.O. "In our heartfelt connections, we put our prosperity in the possession of someone else, which is a really terrifying suggestion. What's more, it surely assists with realizing that your individual will show up for you when things get somewhat unnerving.

For what reason is it vital to assemble trust?

Trust is the establishment for such countless parts of a strong relationship and investing the effort to make that bond will bring about you feeling more joyful and safer as a couple generally. "All the other things feel somewhat more straightforward and more secure when there's trust," On that note, here are a few explicit reasons building trust in relationships is significant:

1. It diminishes struggle.

Everybody needs to feel quiet and agreeable in their relationship and not right while you're snuggling on the love seat, marathon watching your #1 TV show. In any case, you realize what doesn't develop harmony? Feeling like you should screen all that your accomplice is doing, or restlessly considering what they're doing when you're not together. The more those increased feelings assemble, the more certain they are to emerge at a badly arranged time. (What's more, by then, typically imparted in a not exactly useful manner.)

Successful tips to follow:

Have Open Communication

At the point when you work on speaking with your accomplice you discover that you become more open. On the off chance that you become more happy with being open, you become more powerless and foster a more profound relationship - restricting overthinking and disdain in the relationship. Trust can be assembled when your accomplice realizes that you will share close subtleties. You have high expectations about doing as such to fabricate a more grounded association.

2. Be Vulnerable

Weakness can be unnerving, as you might feel judged. Being open to your accomplice assists you with building that trust by demonstrating the way that you can share your most hallowed sentiments. You can let your watchman down and you can act naturally, which thus will cause your accomplice to feel trust in you.

3. Learn Healthy Ways to Communicate

Learning better approaches to impart incorporates undivided attention, approving your accomplice and perceiving how you respond and answer. Couples can peruse relationship books and complete exercise manuals together as ways of reinforcing their trust. Learning better correspondence procedures together forms trust and shows your accomplice your relationship matters.

4. Be Honest

It takes more work to lie than to simply talk about your thoughts. In any event, when it is extreme, being straightforward tells your accomplice that you esteem them. Trust develops when you have a solid sense of reassurance that your accomplice can come clean in any circumstance.

5. Show Empathy

Showing sympathy is a method for causing your accomplice to feel appreciated and approved. Compassion assists with bringing you closer by showing everyday encouragement. On the off chance that your accomplice figures you don't have sympathy they will feel like they're all alone. Particularly assuming you're dating somebody with uneasiness or another emotional well-being concern, showing that you're tuning in and feeling for what they're talking about is significant. Trust is worked from detecting that association.

6. Be Willing to Listen

By paying attention to your accomplice, you are showing them you figure them out. You are showing that you esteem them and you regard them enough to take that time. At the point when you don't pay attention to your accomplice, they might feel excused.

7. Request Clarity if necessary

At the point when you request lucidity, you are showing your accomplice that you care about what they are talking about. In the event that you don't request lucidity, you are left to accept and this might lead you to think awful. Lucidity permits you to distinguish what your accomplice is feeling so you can change ways of behaving. Trust can be fabricated when you request clearness and show your accomplice that you can put forth a valiant effort to address their issues.

8. Try not to Make Assumptions

Suppositions can make a misleading story. At the point when you make a misleading story, you feel eliminated from the association in your relationship. Trust is fabricated when you find an opportunity to get familiar with your accomplice. In the event that you excuse your accomplice's sentiments and put your own contemplations on the circumstance through supposition, you are botching a valuable chance to fabricate a more profound association. Suspicions can make a more destructive story in light of your sentiments. Give your accomplice an opportunity to make sense of and afterward you both can make the consummation of the story together.

9. Set aside some margin to Make Decisions

Taking as much time as is needed to go with choices can permit you to handle your sentiments and attempt to figure out those sentiments and ways of behaving. By dialing back your reaction, you might lessen hurtful incautious choices. This can assist with building trust so your accomplice doesn't feel like you are absent in the midst of contention. They will figure out how to trust you by realizing that you will be there to settle on choices all together.

10. Try not to Take Your Relationship for Granted

At the point when you underestimate your relationship you show your accomplice they don't make any difference. You might put companions before your accomplice when you figure your accomplice will continuously be there. Zeroing in on your accomplice, seeing nice thoughts, and in any event, saying thank you can assist with building trust. Showing enthusiasm for your accomplice prompts building trust.

11. Show Gratitude

Appreciation can be a straightforward type of recognition. Let your accomplice know that you perceive something good they said or did that causes them to feel regarded. Showing appreciation by sending little messages over the course of the day can assist with building trust in a relationship by remaining genuinely associated. A basic signal can go the distance. It shows them you are considering them during your bustling day and this assists with building the strength and confidence in your relationship.

12. Focus on Quality Time

With daily existence and how occupied one can get, quality time can be overlooked. Make a unique opportunity in your day to pause and say howdy or put in no time flat together to assist with building trust. Along these lines, you are telling your accomplice that you will be there to interface regardless of how occupied you get.

13. Put down Stopping points

Limits are rules and cutoff points you set for yourself in your relationship. At the point when you know about unfortunate and solid limits you are more disposed to take responsibility for your activities. At the point several sets limits, they are establishing an agreeable and adjusted climate where the two individuals feel comprehended. At the point when you have a real sense of safety to express no to something, then, at that point, you are defining solid limits. Imparting your own limits to your accomplice assists with building trust.

14. Regard Each Other

Regard shows your accomplice that you will get them how you need to be dealt with. We as a whole enter associations with assumptions and principles of characteristics we believe that our accomplice should have. Trust breaks in the event that we don't communicate similar regard and norms to our accomplices.

15. Set Boundaries

Limits are rules and cutoff points you set for yourself in your relationship. At the point when you know about undesirable and sound limits you are more disposed to take responsibility for your activities. At the point several sets limits, they are establishing an agreeable and adjusted climate where the two individuals feel comprehended. At the point when you have a good sense of safety to express no to something, then you are defining sound limits. Imparting your own limits to your accomplice assists with building trust.

16. Regard Each Other

Regard shows your accomplice that you will get them how you need to be dealt with. We as a whole enter associations with assumptions and guidelines of characteristics we believe our accomplice should have. Trust breaks on the off chance that we don't communicate similar regard and norms to our accomplices.

17. Practice Trust Exercises

At the point when couples set aside some margin to rehearse trust, they feel more associated. Through training, couples can figure out how to assemble trust by turning out to be more open and defenseless. Rehearsing trust practices together shows your accomplice you need to invest the energy.

Trust activities can be things like:

Having cozy discussions.

Giving actual touch.

Having a Q & A period.

Sharing appreciation and praises.

- Giving full attention

Cherishing somebody is regular work. Indeed, I'm calling it a task since you need to genuinely focus on steady consideration in a relationship.

Also, how?

Regardless of whether you need to just let it out, cherishing somebody, seeing someone, the affection, arranging shocks, having intercourse, doing the dishes, managing family, being a group - every last bit of it is a lot of work.

You wind up disappointed in light of the fact that you feel like you're not standing out from your beau or sweetheart or companion.

In any case, in the event that you are honored and things are going without a hitch, this work might appear to be easy. You probably won't actually see it; it will be your natural. What's more, in the event that you love the individual profoundly, you will very much want to offer consideration in a relationship and do as such without it appearing to be an errand.

Nonetheless, as a relationship goes through various stages and tensions of obligations start to mount, really focusing on connections can start to appear to be increasingly difficult.

What occurs, in any case, when the organization/group isn't in a state of harmony?

The matter of cherishing somebody turns out to be adversely effortful and one or the two players begin to feel an absence of consideration in a relationship. Does that imply that you've to simply come to terms with an unfulfilling association? Not really. By putting forth a cognizant attempt to put additional time and consideration in a relationship, you can make something happen.

Things being what they are, the reason do we offer such a lot of significance to consideration in a relationship? Is focusing on detail in connections actually that significant of all things considered? Indeed, to be sure it is on the grounds that not standing out seeing someone leaves your accomplice feeling disliked and neglected.

This carries us to another fundamental inquiry: how would you really focus in a relationship?

To respond to that, first, let us let you know the consideration in a relationship definition.

It implies seeing your accomplice and looking into their life. There are various sorts of considerations in a relationship that you can use to ensure your accomplice sees that you're taking a functioning revenue in their life and are putting resources into what's the deal with them.

These reach from profound consideration, where you're on top of their feelings to general mindfulness, where you don't cover your face in your telephone when your accomplice approaches you to let you know something significant, and heartfelt consideration, where you give them love and warmth.

In the cutting edge world, because of our reliance on contraptions and the requirement for performing various tasks, we end up not having the option to focus on our accomplices. In the event that you have gone out for supper, the very smart arrangement is to keep your telephone inside your pack or pocket.

Be that as it may, without a second to spare, the supervisor says there would be a significant call so you continue squirming with it, anticipating the call.

This could be irritating to your accomplice yet they can't utter a word since work will be work. Without you in any event, acknowledging it, innovation can demolish your relationship. Along these lines, our way of behaving frequently negatively affects correspondence in a relationship.

We are most frequently there truly with our accomplice yet intellectually we are ticking off daily agendas.

So we can't really focus on a relationship.

Toward the end of the day's end, the whole custom of being a couple is just worth the effort when you both have affection toward one another. That can happen exclusively by focusing on somebody you love. Assuming that is feeling the loss of, the customs that are intended to bring you closer and reinforce your bond become useless and the relationship begins to bite the dust.

Once in a while it's the start of the end, and in some cases it is the admonition which when noticed restores a relationship.

All things considered, we experience passionate feelings for one another and become integrated in different common agreements, not exclusively to reproduce yet in addition to friendship and numerous different things. Furthermore, what use is this friendship on the off chance that you're not being mindful of seeing someone? We need observers to our lives and need to be seen and heard, and accomplices do that for one another.

There are billions of us and our lives could lose all sense of direction in that turmoil, yet the way that our accomplice sees our lives, records it, lives it with us makes the entire thing advantageous. It likewise makes all the difference for the correspondence in a relationship. All in all, if in the midst of all that you feel like you're not definitely standing out from sweetheart/sweetheart, why? So assuming you feel that you can't concentrate completely on your accomplice this is what you ought to do.

How Do You Give Someone Attention In A Relationship?

By the end of the day's end, the whole custom of being a couple is just worth the effort when you both have affection toward one another. That can happen exclusively by focusing on somebody you love.

Assuming that is feeling the loss of, the ceremonies that are intended to bring you closer and fortify your bond become worthless and the relationship begins to pass on. At times it's the start of the end, and once in a while it is the admonition which when noticed resuscitates a relationship.

All things considered, we experience passionate feelings for one another and become integrated in various common agreements, not exclusively to reproduce yet in addition to friendship and numerous different things. Furthermore, what use is this friendship in the event that you're not being mindful of seeing someone? We need observers to our lives and need to be seen and heard, and accomplices do that for one another.

1. Grasp focusing the implicit promise.

full focus in connections

Consideration is significant seeing someone

What happens then when our accomplices remove that seeing? That is the point at which a relationship begins to flame out and accomplices will more often than not turn away from one another.

Your consideration goes to various things when you feel the absence of consideration in a relationship. That is the point at which your association winds up in peril. As may be obvious, not definitely standing out seeing someone has sweeping ramifications for your future as a couple.

This, obviously, is certainly not a cognizant cycle without fail, however even the oblivious dismissing can be seriously pernicious in a relationship. Giving unified consideration to one another is the implicit promise that couples take when they get together.

Nobody falls head over heels since they find the other individual exhausting.

Experiencing passionate feelings makes individuals find their accomplices intriguing, regardless of whether others think they are exhausting.

I'm not recommending that our accomplices are our wellsprings of diversion, yet they should be fascinating assuming we will enjoy our lives with them.

2. It cuts further than we could see

To this end an accomplice overlooking you can sting so much, to a certain extent where individuals get discouraged and even contemplate taking their lives. Since their sweethearts quit seeing them as well as on the grounds that that absence of seeing dissolves importance out of their lives.

At the point when the individual you care most about, the person who's your daylight and starlight, quits thinking that you are intriguing, it can make you question your reality.

That is the reason a mindful accomplice makes you blissful and a careless one makes you dour. Not getting time and consideration in that frame of mind from your accomplice can be a desolate encounter.

Certain individuals love with their entire being, they pull out all the stops and overlook every one of their cards. For their purposes, this bet merits the award.

Normal rules don't apply in this situation. They let it all out, in light of the fact that for them adoring somebody that way feels inauthentic.

Regardless of whether you love along these lines, when the other individual removes their adoration subsequent to giving it for quite a while, it delivers a void.

This void can be difficult and wrestling with it is difficult and they might in fact get clinically discouraged in such a circumstance. Consequently, focusing on detail in connections turns into even more significant. It further develops correspondence in a relationship.

3. Cultural shame demolishes what is going on

This turns out to be much more risky when we consider that our general public disparages psychological instability and examining our feelings is viewed as a pointless demonstration. For a general public that laps up romantic comedy dramas, we sure are quiet and critical about our own feelings.

Individuals frequently go to therapists to discuss how their accomplices don't offer them consideration yet they can't see their accomplices they feel disregarded.

Thus, on the off chance that not standing out from a sweetheart or mate can be this unsafe and consideration in a relationship can hold such a lot of importance, the two accomplices must hold up the responsibility of focusing on each other, not simply during the thrilling special night period of the relationship however each and every day.

What's the significance here to be mindful of seeing someone?

In this way, we've demonstrated that not definitely standing out seeing someone is unfavorable to your security. It's significantly more vital to comprehend how precisely we can be mindful seeing someone and what does being mindful seeing someone mean. How might you be more thoughtful in a relationship?

Being mindful of seeing someone is something remarkable to every relationship dynamic. For certain couples, being mindful can mean being mindful of your accomplice's temperaments while for others it can just mean making them their #1 food to show they give it a second thought.

The thought is to be insightful toward your accomplice's singular necessities and not let your bond as a team debilitate. Being mindful is just our method for showing our accomplices we give it a second thought and cause them to feel significant and unique.

They hold a unique spot in our lives and being mindful of them shows them that.

Consequently, the absence of consideration in a relationship can likewise hold an alternate importance for various couples. Obliviousness and not focusing on detail in connections can show themselves in various ways in a relationship.

For one couple, not saying 'I love you' toward the beginning of the day can hold as much weight as effectively disregarding the accomplice. So how would you focus closer? How might you be more mindful of your significant other or spouse or accomplice? We should sort it out.

Why Is Attention Important In A Relationship?

These reach from close to home consideration, where you're on top of their feelings to general mindfulness, where you don't cover your face in your telephone when your accomplice approaches you to let you know something significant, and heartfelt consideration, where you give them love and friendship.

This, obviously, is certainly not a cognizant cycle without fail, however even the oblivious dismissing can be seriously terrible in a relationship. Giving unified consideration to one another is the implicit promise that couples take when they get together. Nobody becomes hopelessly enamored in light of the fact that they find the other individual exhausting.

Experiencing passionate feelings makes individuals find their accomplices intriguing, regardless of whether others think they are exhausting. I'm not proposing that our accomplices are our wellsprings of diversion, however they should be fascinating assuming we will enjoy our lives with them.

daylight and starlight, quits thinking that you are fascinating, it can make you question your reality. That is the reason a mindful accomplice makes you cheerful and a careless one makes you bleak. Not getting time and consideration in that frame of mind from your accomplice can be a desolate encounter.

Certain individuals love with their entire being, they go all in and overlook every one of their cards. For their purposes, this bet merits the prize. Normal rules don't apply in this situation. They let it all out, in light of the fact that for them cherishing somebody that way feels inauthentic.

Regardless of whether you love along these lines, when the other individual removes their adoration in the wake of giving it for quite a while, it delivers a void. This void can be difficult and wrestling with it is difficult and they could get clinically discouraged in such a circumstance. Hence, focusing on detail in connections turns into even more significant. It further develops correspondence in a relationship.

Individuals frequently go to specialists to discuss how their accomplices don't offer them consideration yet they can't perceive their accomplices they feel dismissed.

Thus, on the off chance that not definitely standing out from a sweetheart or mate can be this unsafe and consideration in a relationship can hold such a lot of importance, the two accomplices must hold up the responsibility of focusing on each other, not simply during the thrilling special first night period of the relationship yet each and every day.

4. Fail to focus on correspondence

In long haul connections, individuals become so immersed in the errands, youngsters and covering the bills that they fail to focus on correspondence. They could be watching a film together on the lounge room love seat, however they just focus on the popcorn. There is an absence of correspondence in a relationship then.

Keeping each other side by side of what's going on in one another's lives is an approach to focusing completely on the accomplice. You really want to discuss your day, your children, make occasion arrangements and even cook together.

Correspondence securities individuals and you don't feel disregarded assuming you are imparting great.

In the event that there is a slip by correspondence in your relationship, you could attempt to work it out.

What's the significance here to be mindful of seeing someone?

In this way, we've demonstrated that not definitely standing out seeing someone is hindering your security. It's considerably more pivotal to comprehend how precisely we can be mindful seeing someone and what does being mindful seeing someone mean.

How might you be more obliging in a relationship?

Being mindful of seeing someone is something special to every relationship dynamic. For certain couples, being mindful can mean being mindful of your accomplice's mind-sets while for others it can essentially mean making them their #1 food to show they give it a second thought. The thought is to be keen toward your accomplice's singular necessities and not let your bond as a team debilitate.

Being mindful is essentially our method for showing our accomplices we give it a second thought and cause them to feel significant and extraordinary. They hold an extraordinary spot in our lives and being mindful of them shows them that. Subsequently, the absence of consideration in a relationship can likewise hold an alternate significance for various couples.

Obliviousness and not focusing on detail in connections can show themselves in various ways in a relationship. For one couple, not saying 'I love you' toward the beginning of the day can hold as much weight as effectively disregarding the accomplice.

So how would you focus closer? How might you be more mindful of your significant other or spouse or accomplice? How about we sort it out.

How would I focus harder on my accomplice?

Despite the fact that each relationship is remarkable, you can in any case detect that your sweetheart/accomplice feels that you're not being mindful when seeing someone. Assuming that occurs, the following are a couple of things you can do to cure what is happening by focusing on somebody you love: A mindful individual satisfies his accomplice.

Tune in: Listening is significant in any relationship. A great deal of times we hear our accomplice however don't actually stand by listening to them which can cause them to feel like they're not definitely standing out seeing someone.

Make arrangements with one another:

Customarily, the steady drudgery of a routine can cause it to feel like all that in your life is stale, including your relationship. You can feel like you're not standing out from your accomplice. To get through the dreariness, you can make arrangements with each other, which can be basically as straightforward as a home-prepared supper date or a film date

Try not to avoid their complaints: You might feel like your accomplice continually whines about similar issues, yet don't excuse their complaints. On the off chance that you do this they can feel an unmistakable absence of consideration from your end.

Cause them to feel unique:

Recollect the days where you assumed you had found your perfect partner? Indeed, this is a similar individual, and they have the right to feel exceptional. Plan heartfelt date evenings or reproduce an old date you had. This makes certain to fix your accomplice of the absence of consideration blues.

Plan an outing:

Nothing can be better for a drawn out relationship restoration than a get-away for two which offers you the chance to unwind, loosen up and manufacture nearer bonds.

Speak with them:

Correspondence is much of the time the way to rescuing most connections. It helps in getting out any questions, consoling and supporting your affection for one another.

In this way, utilize these correspondence tips for more viable correspondence.

What we should really try to understand is that there's a feeling of being abandoned that individuals can feel when there is an absence of consideration in connections.

Free and open exchange needs to turn into a customary movement. It's additionally similarly critical to teach ourselves about psychological wellness and furthermore discuss the developing types of marriage and close connections.

While each adoration experience is exceptional and abstract, there are fundamental principles of the game that we can impart to one another.

We want to show individuals how to convey so they continue to observe one another.

Assuming adoration drives everything and everyone, clear correspondence moves love along around and we really want a greater amount of that. Particularly in connections where a reasonable absence of full focus can be felt.

- Making amend

More often than not, we compare offering to set things right with saying 'sorry' Be that as it may, there is something else to it besides trying to say sorry. Setting things right is tied in with making things right. It's the longing to recuperate broken connections. The last part, specifically, makes it more troublesome.

Connections resemble delicate fires. When it breaks, it's difficult to reestablish it back to what it used to be. Indeed, you can fix it up and stick the pieces back together. However, the breaks will in any case be apparent. In any case, that doesn't mean you shouldn't basically attempt to return the wrecked pieces. Indeed, attempting to fix a messed up relationship is definitely not a simple errand. Indeed, even the demonstration of saying you're heartbroken and confessing to our missteps takes an unbelievable measure of mental fortitude.

Be that as it may, assuming you truly are earnest in your expectation to fix things, no undertaking is excessively overwhelming. Plus, the choice to set things right with individuals you've harmed is now a major step. On the off chance that you're as yet not certain how to continue, here are a few hints on the most proficient method to offer to set things straight and begin recuperating broken relationships:

1.Permit Yourself To Be Vulnerable

Opening yourself up and making yourself powerless may be the hardest thing you'll at any point do. In any case, being straightforward with yourself and the individual you've harmed is the initial step to recuperating. Since adolescence, we've been designed to suppress our feelings. There's consistently that idea that bearing everything to all onlookers makes you look feeble. This is the main obstacle that you really want to survive.

To set things right, you want to let the other individual know what you truly feel. Tell them your second thoughts and your expectations. This will assist the other individual with figuring out your side of the story. Spill your guts and cry however much you need. It won't make you a lesser individual. All things considered, it makes you such a great deal more grounded.

2. Wonder Why You Are Making Amends

For what reason would you like to set things right? Might it be said that you are simply helping it since you really want out from the other individual? Or on the other hand is it since you truly need to fix things up with them? Assuming that you're doing this without regard for anyone else, you might have to reconsider your expectations. At some point or another, the other individual will understand what you're really doing. What's more, when that occurs, you might in all likelihood won't ever have.

3. Think about The Reason For The Fallout

Most broken connections aren't brought about by a solitary struggle. A consequence of numerous neglected little issues gathered momentum into what it is presently. So before you request pardoning, ponder what really caused the contention. Was it due to a new squabble? Or on the other hand is it due to basic issues that you both overlooked until it made a huge deal about? Knowing the genuine justification behind the aftermath will assist you with expressing yourself. Assuming you remember those purposes behind your expression of remorse, it will likewise show the other individual that you truly are genuine about setting things right.

4. Apologize Sincerely.

A conciliatory sentiment, if not genuine, is only an exercise in futility. The other individual might acknowledge it yet it can never fix things up between both of you. It will simply resemble putting a bandage on a rotting wound. For a statement of regret to accomplish its motivation, it should come from the heart. You don't require such a large number of words or excellent motions. You simply have to show genuine regret for what you've done.

5. Bring down Your Pride

More often than not, when we apologize, we will generally accuse others as opposed to taking ownership of our mix-ups. This is pride working. In the event that you truly believe the other individual should feel your genuineness, bring down your pride. Acknowledge that you are somewhat flawed and that you are likewise equipped for committing errors. Rather than faulting others for your terrible choices, own ready. It doesn't damage to say, "I was off-base. Please accept my apologies." Well, aside from a swollen self image obviously. Be that as it may, you'll make due.

6. Try not to Make Excuses

Committing pardons for your errors is similarly pretty much as awful as accusing others. At the point when you apologize, simply apologize. Try not to attempt to rationalize. On the off chance that you do, you are legitimizing your activities as opposed to requesting absolution. How, then, might the other individual at any point excuse you?

7. Pay attention to Their Side of the Story

Making an expression of remorse ought to be a two-way road. You air your side yet you ought to likewise allow the other individual an opportunity to say their piece as well. Pay attention to their side of the story and comprehend how they feel. Who knows, it could provide you with a new viewpoint of the circumstance.

8. Come at the situation from the Other Person's Perspective

Some of the time, we just need to set things right with somebody since we realize we've harmed them. Yet, we have no clue about how much hurt we've caused until we imagine their perspective. Attempt to see things according to their perspective. Assuming that they've done to you all that you've done to them, how might you have felt? Assuming you are forced to bear the conciliatory sentiment you're making at present, will you track down it in your heart to pardon?

9. Ask How You Can Make Things Right

After you've apologized, ask the other individual how you can make things right. This will tell them that you truly mean to compensate for what you did.

10. Give The Other Person Time and Space to Process Your Apology.

If saying sorry is hard, it is significantly more enthusiastic to acknowledge one. You can't anticipate that somebody should pardon you since you apologized. Particularly assuming they went through a few genuinely horrendous things as a result of you. You really want to give them existence to acknowledge your expression of remorse. Try not to compel them to answer immediately. It might require months or years so you should show restraint. Recollect that they are going through their very own course as well.

11. Give Them Time to Heal

Assuming the individual you've harmed acknowledges your conciliatory sentiment, that doesn't imply that things can return to how they were. Recuperating, whether physical or close to home, takes time particularly in the event that the injury is excessively profound. Assuming they excuse you, be appreciative of it. In any case, don't constrain them to simply continue on and carry on as though nothing occurred. Allow them an opportunity to recuperate. It's the least you can do.

12. Keep to Your Purpose

Excusing somebody takes a great deal of mental fortitude. So don't be astounded on the off chance that certain individuals can't track down it in that frame of mind to pardon you. It's their privilege. Try not to allow it to deter you from setting things straight with others. The significant thing is you've requested their absolution and will improve.

Chapter 2

HANDLING RELATIONSHIP ISSUES

Each and every individual who decides to be seeing someone experience issues in their relationship now and again. Whether enormous or little, we can figure out how to manage relationship issues through sound correspondence, shared regard, and split the difference. It's great for accomplices to figure out how to talk about relationship issues without battling, and to attempt to determine relationship issues without separating. Nonetheless, there might be times when contrasts or irritating issues lead to a separation. It is vital to comprehend how to manage relationship problems and when it very well might be an ideal opportunity to leave.

Probably the most well-known issues that cause struggle inside a relationship are:

- Outside Intimacy

The fact that many couples battle with makes sex and closeness one more issue. Accomplices might have various requirements and wants around actual closeness. One individual might need sex more frequently than the other, or might be more open to various children of sex or having intercourse with more than one individual, like in open or polyamorous connections. times there are confusions in solace levels with public presentations of love one accomplice probably shouldn't be truly warm openly while different does. Also, these inclinations might change over the long haul as the relationship advances.Continuous and fair sharing about closeness necessities and inclinations is a centerpiece of keeping a relationship solid.

It's memorable's critical that assent is really significant in a sexual relationship. Assent should be:

Excited: You and your accomplice ought to communicate that you need to be participating in sexual movement.

Willful: You shouldn't feel compelled in any capacity to take part in sexual movement.

Informed: Understand what the sexual action includes, and what any potential outcomes are.

Explicit: Consent can be given for one sexual action however not others. Before you attempt various exercises, check in about how your accomplice is feeling.

Progressing: Saying yes to sex one time doesn't mean you have consented to each sexual experience. Check in before each time you need to be truly cozy. To draw nearer to your accomplice and to establish a climate for energetic assent in your relationship, think about planning "date evenings," or confidential time where you lose your standard schedules and accomplish something you partake in together. You shouldn't feel constrained into sex or any sexual action to keep up with your relationship. Feeling constrained, forced, or coerced into sex isn't assent.

- Career planning and finance

At the point when the two accomplices in a relationship work, offsetting love with career can be troublesome. Present day sentiment frequently implies nobody is home to make supper, and quality time can be elusive.

The following are 10 methods for stilling make progress as a team while seeking after a profession:

1. Put down stopping points. Whether it's the time you each leave the workplace, or how frequently you telecommute, ensure you convey and set clear assumptions regarding how your professions will seep into your life. Make a standard that you can't take a gander at iPhones after 7:00 pm, or that you'll both work on Sunday evenings. Vocation arranged couples frequently appreciate working, yet defining limits permits you to likewise partake in one another.

2. Talk funds early and frequently. The most well-known contention couples face is around cash. So talk now, while things are great, on whether every individual will uphold the other on the off chance that an employment is lost or on the other hand assuming another vocation course is liked. Is it true that you will plunge into your investment funds to help a migration? How might your way of life change in the event that your accomplice gets an advancement? Conclude how you will distribute cash at home and for work.

3. Cut opportunities for one another. It's essential to make customary chances to spend time together. Perhaps you make exceptional minutes out of getting things done or maybe you practice each Saturday together. You can likewise take a stab at booking a night out on the town for each Tuesday that can't be rescheduled. The point is to figure out quality opportunities together to anticipate.

4. Try not to hit the sack furious. A familiar aphorism that is significant for the progress of both your relationship and your profession. Assuming that you awaken irate, besides the fact that you conceivably wasted important time from the prior night, yet you likewise get a negative beginning to your morning that can influence your efficiency over the course of the day. Figure out your problems before your head raises a ruckus around town to ultimately benefit your relationship and your vocation

5. Balance penances. To seek after a high-profile profession, very nearly an assurance penances should be made to ultimately benefit that vocation. Recall that equilibrium is made over significant stretches of time. Acknowledge and recognize the significance of your accomplice's penance to additional your vocation and do likewise for their fantasies from now on.

6. Show unrestricted help. Showing interest in your companion's profession following some serious time work can be troublesome. Yet, it's critical that you're smart and present in your discussions connecting with your accomplice's vocation, and that your help is unqualified toward their work. Without such help, an absence of understanding and disdain can raise in your accomplice, making it hard to go about as a couple.

7. Love the individual, not their title. For the soundness of your relationship, ensure you've gone gaga for your accomplice personally, and not with their title or position. In the present economy, nothing is sure, and similarity is not generally founded on whether the other individual can deal with you. All things being equal, realize that you can deal with yourself, and choose if you actually need your accomplice around.

8. Do the choice two-step. The initial step to pursuing a choice is you, and the second is your accomplice. Never again are you working in life freely, regardless of how determined your character is. Your choices currently influence one another, and you need to perceive your accomplice has equivalent say. Set yourself up to deal with the results of the other individual's activities.

9. Share family obligations. Nobody needs to return home to a sink loaded with messy dishes. Evenly dividing family tasks is much of the time a staying point between couples that grows into continuous contentions. Allocate clear jobs and conclude who makes a garbage run, who does the dishes, who cooks, and who vacuums. Stick to it, however at that point don't hesitate for even a moment to break out the dish cleanser when your accomplice is having an extreme week.

10. Excuse and apologize

In a universe of vocation vulnerability, connections can be a protected establishment and minimizer of stress. Try not to make things more troublesome by holding hard feelings. Discuss frequently with your accomplice; show sympathy toward their awful mind-sets and praise their great ones. A fruitful relationship is in many cases the most important move toward an effective vocation. Ensure you focus on the big picture approach.

Ultimately, Cash is quite possibly the most well-known issue that causes struggle in a relationship. Whether it's having different monetary assets, various perspectives about the significance of cash, or different ways of managing money, cash issues can cause strain in a relationship. This is particularly obvious assuming that there is a lopsidedness of force for instance, when one accomplice has more monetary assets and feels like they "owe" their accomplice monetarily.

Here are far to determine expected clashes about funds:

Speak the truth about your monetary circumstance. Clear the air regarding what you can and can't manage the cost of concerning dates and gifts.

Try not to involve cash as influence or "ammo" during battles or conflicts that are not about cash. Assuming you live respectively and choose to join funds, split the difference about spending and saving propensities in a manner that is reasonable for the two individuals.

Have separate monetary records from each other. This keeps things fair, yet it tends to be a significant piece of a compelling wellbeing plan on the off chance that the relationship closes.

- Trust and jealousy

Feeling shaky, desirous, or wary in a relationship can prompt various issues rapidly particularly in the event that there are clear explanations behind the doubt. In some cases, these sentiments emerge when there is not a glaringly obvious explanation. A large number of us feel uncertain in a relationship since we don't have a lot of relationship experience, have areas of low self-esteem that influence how we feel about ourselves in a relationship, or in light of the fact that we have irritating issues from a past relationship. Assuming that you perceive that your sensations of weakness are coming from inside yourself, consider talking it through with your accomplice or looking for help from a specialist who can assist you with focusing on the heart of the matter.

In different occurrences, your accomplice's activities or words can cause sensations of weakness, either deliberately or coincidentally. Assuming you feel as such, check in with your accomplice. Having legit discussions about hard themes like this are unavoidable in solid connections and can be strong chances to develop as a team and as people. Nonetheless, assuming your accomplice over and again excuses your interests, limits their frightful way of behaving, or leaves you feeling more terrible instead of consoled after you talk, it very well might be an ideal opportunity to leave the relationship.

- Managing friendships and other people

Having a relationship with your accomplice is a magnificent, useful excursion, yet at last, it becomes hard to similarly keep up with both relationships and kinships! Whether you're losing contact with your companions or focusing more on your companions than your accomplice, this article will assist you with tracking down a good overall arrangement between both your affection life and companions' time. Make a stride back and view your relationship with your accomplice and your different fellowships. In some cases, you may not be investigating the entire picture; you might be simply zeroing in on one piece of your nursery and dismissing every one of the weeds filling in different spots!

Pose yourself these inquiries:

Am I investing sufficient energy with both to shape significant bonds truly?

Who am I with more often than not?

Are there additional good or pessimistic sentiments in my accomplice's relationship and my kinships?

Do I feel discontent with my relationship or kinships?

Think about sentiments.

Do you detect negative energy from your accomplice or companions? On the off chance that there is by all accounts a cloudier strain in your relationship, you might need to lay off some time from spending time with your companions. Assuming that it's the reverse way around, you might be investing a lot of energy in your adoration life. Converse with your accomplice and companions, if conceivable, and ask them how they feel.

Do you invest a lot of energy keeping an eye on your relationship and dismissing the weeds in your kinships, or is it the reverse way around? You can't simply zero in on one piece of the nursery, yet you should investigate the entire nursery. Where are the weeds flourishing more?

Consider what your needs lay.

Is it your life, companions, profession, and so forth? Despite the fact that you have your relationship and fellowships to keep an eye on, you should zero in on your needs, yet not such a lot that you are dismissing your accomplice and companions! Spread your time so you can be with every individual actually.

Recollect that you can't be wherever without a moment's delay; there is only one of you, so time matters in this step! Using time effectively is significant in keeping up with both relationships and fellowships. It's basic to give time to your accomplice, your pals, and - in particular yourself! Realize that your accomplice is similarly essentially as significant as your companions. Nobody merits more consideration than the other.

Continuously be in contact. Seeing someone means you can't spend time with your mates. Spend time with them no less than one time per week; in the event that you can't be available, sending them a card telling them you love them is more contacting than an email or instant message.

Go out on an excursion with your companions. Whether it's an excursion to the club, bowling, or a dinner at a café, make the most of each and every second! Never forget about one of your companions!

Know about what is happening in your companions' lives. In the event that you don't refresh yourself on their status like clockwork, they will figure you could do without them and your kinships will shrink!

Going on friendly sites like Facebook, Twitter, Myspace, and so on can assist you with staying in contact with your companions. Also, you can undoubtedly design get-togethers and gather hang outs!

Having a relationship with your accomplice is a magnificent, useful excursion, yet at last, it becomes hard to similarly keep up with both relationships and kinships! Whether you're losing contact with your companions or focusing more on your companions than your accomplice, this article will assist you with tracking down a good overall arrangement between both your adoration life and companions' time.

Taking into account Your Thoughts

Make a stride back and view your relationship with your accomplice and your different companionships. In some cases, you may not be investigating the entire picture; you might be simply zeroing in on one piece of your nursery and ignoring every one of the weeds filling in different spots! Pose yourself these inquiries:

Am I investing sufficient energy with both to shape significant bonds truly?

Who am I with more often than not?

Are there additional good or gloomy sentiments in my accomplice's relationship and my fellowships?

Do I feel discontent with my relationship or kinships?

Think about sentiments. Do you detect negative energy from your accomplice or companions? On the off chance that there is by all accounts a cloudier strain in your relationship, you might need to lay off some time from spending time with your companions. Assuming that it's the opposite way around, you might be investing a lot of energy in your adoration life

Converse with your accomplice and companions, if conceivable, and ask them how they feel. Do you invest an excess of energy watching out for your relationship and dismissing the weeds in your fellowships, or is it the opposite way around? You can't simply zero in on one piece of the nursery, however you should investigate the entire nursery.

Consider what your needs lay. Is it your life, companions, vocation, and so on? Despite the fact that you have your relationship and kinships to watch out for, you should zero in on your needs, however not so much that you are dismissing your accomplice and companions! Spread your time so you can be with every individual by and by. Recall that you can't be wherever without a moment's delay; there is only one of you, so time matters in this step!

Using time productively is significant in keeping up with both relationships and kinships. It's basic to give time to your accomplice, your pals, and in particular yourself! Realize that your accomplice is similarly pretty much as significant as your companions. Nobody merits more consideration than the other.

Ensure your accomplice knows about the times you intend to spend time with your companions or have private time alone. Along these lines, your timetable and your accomplice's timetable won't be vexed. In the event that your accomplice has no clue about your gathering hang out and designs an exceptional shock supper for you that day, without a doubt he/she will be harmed! Telling your accomplice about your timetable will forestall any put in an awful mood and disarray from here on out.

Ensure your accomplice is likewise mindful of who your companions are. It's best that he/she knows who your companions are so there is no concern of who you're spending time with. This will likewise delete any possessive or concerned sentiments in your accomplice.

Recall that you are committed, not banned in a relationship. Ensure your companions know about that also. They need to realize that you love your accomplice's organization, yet you miss their organization also. You can in any case carry on with your life anyway you need; your accomplice has no control over you around there. You settle on the choices

Allow your accomplice to do their things as they need. Try not to be the over-possessive accomplice since the person has more young ladies or fellow companions. Assuming that your accomplice truly focuses on you, he/she won't undermine you. Notwithstanding, being certain that you truly do invest sufficient energy with your accomplice will keep your accomplice from holding such contemplations.

Assuming your accomplice undermines you, realize that it isn't your issue. Your accomplice likely feels denied affection and sees something different in someone else that he/she doesn't find in you.

Ensure you are there when your dearest companion needs a shoulder to incline or cry on. Along these lines, you should rest assured they will give back in kind in the future when you want them! In any case, assuming that you can't be available, sending them a smart, cherishing card that guarantees your help with them can be similarly essentially as sweet as you being there face to face with them.

Never postpone sending solace or consolation to your companion. Your companion will no doubt hold put in a bad mood and puzzle over regardless of whether you truly are their closest companion.

Make it a point to take a stand in opposition to how you feel, yet think about others' sentiments and do it in the gentlest yet firmest manner. Try not to allow anybody to control you. This is your life, and these are your choices! Do allow individuals to impact your choices a tad, yet don't allow them to pursue the choices for you except if in the event that their recommendation appears to be preferable over your own.

Partake in your thriving nursery of relationship and kinships! Make certain to watch out for it consistently and never disregard one piece of it. Continuously take a gander at the entire picture and take the necessary steps to take out the weeds and keep the blossoms sprouting.